BREATHE LIFE INTO YOUR RESUME

JEANNINE BENNETT

Published in Virginia Beach, Virginia, U.S.A. by Vision to Purpose, LLC. www.visiontopurpose.com

ISBN-13: 978-1702644136 (Paperback edition)

Cover design by Crystal Calhoun, madetobeunique.com
Cover photo by Tero Vesalainen from pixabay.com
Printed in the United States of America.
First Printing: November 2019

Disclaimer: Although the author and publisher have made every effort to ensure that the information in this book was correct at press time, the author and publisher do not assume and hereby disclaims any liability to any party for any loss, damage, or disruption caused by errors or omissions, whether such errors or omissions result from negligence, accident, or any other cause.

The information provided in this book is to be used as a guide only; use at your own risk. There are no guarantees of employment or any other result from reading this book. The author and publisher assumes no responsibility or liability whatsoever on the behalf of the reader of these materials.

I dedicate this book to the many students and clients who, over the years, have asked me to write a book on resume writing to help others. It has been a great joy to know I have helped them succeed in their efforts and it will please me immensely to know I can help you through this book too.

Friends, I am cheering for you!

Sincerely,
Jeannine

RECOMMENDATIONS

Want to know what others have said about the resume writing and career coaching services Jeannine provides, then take a look at the recommendations from some of her clients. You can find a more complete list on her website: www.visiontopurpose.com and on her LinkedIn profile at https://www.linkedin.com/in/jbennettphd/.

"What an awesome experience! Jeannine exceeded my expectations tremendously. Not only did she help write my resume and enhance my LinkedIn profile, she coached me on my career and provided invaluable guidance! I can't thank Jeannine enough for such a professional experience."
Lovey, Assistant Vice President, Financial Industry

"Jeannine is a one-stop shop for transitioning career support. She helped me to not only transition from the military but also facilitated my securing a job in the federal government. Her diverse background has made her an expert in preparing and coaching for interview questions and ensures you are ready to impress. I emphatically trust her career advice and relied on her positive spirit and motivation to keep me focused during the trials of a job search. I will continue to recommend Jeannine to anyone who is in need of a helping hand in navigating the job market." *Jill, Government Civilian, U.S. Navy Veteran, Government Sector*

"My experience working with Jeannine was all-around excellent. She worked with me to renew my resume and add a fresh update to my LinkedIn profile. She was extremely efficient in her communications and got right to work providing several new layouts with creative ways to capture the attention of those who will view your resume. Her insights on my LinkedIn page have also been very helpful. I'd recommend working with Jeannine if you're looking for great results at a great value."
David, Manager, Cyber Governance & Risk Management, Financial Industry

"I am very pleased with the resume/cover letter/LinkedIn profile you updated/created for me. They are very accurate and demonstrate my skills and accomplishments. Your writing is absolutely fantastic! Very organized and professional. I couldn't have done this myself. The turnaround time for my questions/recommendation were quick. You did exactly what you promised you would do. Your pricing is comparable to the market even though your Ph.D. professional work exceeded it! I will not hesitate to recommend you and would definitely reach out to you if I need any additional work to be done." *Kokila, Scrum Master, Defense Industry*

"I found Jeannine through LinkedIn ProFinder as I was searching for someone to help me revamp my resume. Jeannine's work is top notch. I found working with Jeannine to be really productive. Jeannine is really a 'Career Strategist' as she provides ideas, knowledge and is thorough in everything she does. If you are searching for a resume writer, a career coach or a LinkedIn specialist, I highly recommend Jeannine. She is truly a pleasure to work with and will go above and beyond your expectations." *Peggie, Business Strategist & Sales Enabler, Technology Industry*

You can find additional recommendations in the back of the book.

CONTENTS

INTRODUCTION

Does the thought of writing a resume make you cringe? Trust me when I say you are not alone. Most job seekers in today's modern job market do not like to write their resume. In fact, I have clients who are top notch human resources professionals who are trained in writing and finding talent contact me about creating their resumes. Initially, I was perplexed by those calls until I realized the real problem was staring me right in the face. Resume writing is hard but it is not necessarily the writing that's the problem, it's the writing about oneself that gets people stuck.

How many times have you started working on your resume only to lose steam halfway through the process? Probably several, right? The reality is that people have a hard time talking about themselves; trying to put accomplishments into words in a way that conveys their true value to a prospective employer becomes overwhelming. The first attempt at writing a resume usually takes many arduous hours of painstaking work only to be rejected by the writer even before it can make its way to a prospective employer. Defeated, the writer starts over time and time again.

If you have indeed created your own resume, I bet you are not truly happy with it. I can even tell you the process you went through to create it and what you did after you created it. First, you probably looked at every online resume you could find that pertained to your field of expertise. Second, you likely downloaded a couple of sample resumes to make sure you did things right. Third, you probably asked a friend for a copy of their resume as a guide. Fourth, you might have even found some site where you could do a plug and play resume where you basically entered all your data into some database and—presto change-o—out came a pre-formatted resume to use.

It's not that any of those are necessarily 100% wrong. For some people, those might work, but you are not some person. You are unique just like the life you have lived so your resume should be one of a kind too.

I know you are probably thinking, "Jeannine, you have lost your mind. How on earth can I create a one of a kind resume? Don't I have to follow some sort of resume rules?" The answer is yes and no. Yes, employers do want resumes to contain pertinent information to help them determine if you are the right person for the job. However, there are many ways to do that and still conform to some tried and true best practices for resume writing.

Now, I hope I didn't scare you off with the resume writing is hard talk. Remember it is only hard because you are talking about yourself. This book is designed to help you tell your professional career story in a way that makes the process a whole lot easier.

In this book, you will learn how to create a resume that will get you selected over the competition, get you hired by the right company, and get you paid what you are worth. It starts with breathing life into your resume through the unique message you convey and the visual you present. The process is similar to what companies do when they write copy to sell a product. The only difference is that you are the product we want to market to the buyer (aka the prospective employer).

As your story unfolds on your resume, so does your personal brand. From your resume, the prospective employer will be able to see who you are, what you excel in, and what you have to offer.

If you're ready to move forward on your new resume, then let's get started.

As you will see, this book is divided into three parts. The first part is called your message. This is where you will learn what to convey, how to showcase your personal brand, and how to determine your audience.

The second part of the book focuses on putting your story to paper. This is a vital part; it tells you what should be included on your resume. Let's face it, no matter how visually appealing your resume is, you still need *substance*. If your resume lacks substance, then your overall resume will suck. Yes, I said suck. Once the substance is captured, then we tackle the visual side of the resume.

The final part of this book is about preparing your mindset for the job hunt, which can be either a short- or long-term quest. If you do not go into the process of searching for a job with the right mindset you might just sabotage all your good work making your efforts useless. You don't want to work hard on your resume for nothing.

The aim of this guide is not only to help you create an appealing resume, but also to help you create an effective one that highlights your true worth. Resume design isn't so much about looking pretty, it is more about eliminating clutter and enhancing the effectiveness of your professional message to break through the noise and resonate with the reviewer.

Each section will build upon the other until you have enough information to move ahead on crafting a well-designed resume. To ensure nothing is lost while you work toward a final product at the end of each chapter you will find key points of reference of what you learned to keep you on track, plan of action items to keep you accountable and words of wisdom to keep you encouraged through the resume writing process.

If you follow the information provided in this book you will ultimately have both an effective and appealing resume that will help you stand out from your competition and land you that interview.

Finally, additional resources have been provided in the back of this book and via a link to the Bonus Materials found at https://bit.ly/breatheresume.

Resources include:

- Plan of Action Journal to capture your information from each chapter's action items in one location
- Larger illustrations from the book for easier viewing
- Sample resumes to review for ideas
- Resume templates so that you don't have to start from scratch
- List of action verbs to help you craft your bullets
- Resume checklist to ensure you did not forgot anything

I

YOUR MESSAGE

Developing Your Core Message
Building Your Brand
Naming Your Audience

DEVELOPING YOUR CORE MESSAGE

One of the most common mistakes job seekers make happens at the moment a new job opportunity pops and they have to create a resume to apply. They frantically throw together a resume or scramble to revise an old one. In either case, they dump a plethora of information into the resume in hopes that something will stick and with a bit of luck resonate with the job reviewer. The result? A resume that is filled with too much text and very little inspiration. There is no central message found in that resume. It is just a document with some text and a lot of bullets.

Instead, I recommend taking a different approach by including your core resume message. In other words, what are you trying to convey in your resume to anyone who reads it? The core message must be the single most important idea you want the prospective employer to take away after reviewing your resume. What is it that you want the reviewer to remember about you after he or she has read 20 other resumes?

A core message in a resume is simple, it is merely something that tells your audience who you are and what you excel in.

It is no different than reading a book and being drawn to a particular character. Why do you think when you read a book you are drawn to one character over another? It is most likely due to the way the author laid out the story. Perhaps the author wanted you to connect with that character for a reason. Maybe the character was the underdog who, by the end of the story, was the hero. Just as an author writes a book to connect with his or her readers, you need to do the same to connect with your audience, the potential employer.

How do you connect? You weave your real-life story throughout your resume.

Let me be clear, this is a true-life story, not a work of fiction. You must always tell the truth on a resume because falsifying information or fudging the truth won't get you anywhere. Today, there are too many systems in place that can instantly pull information that can and will counter a potential embellishment you may have made, so don't risk it. Everyone has a story to tell, but no one has your exact story.

To get your story right you need to have the facts set before you. The facts can be in the form of an old resume that you are revising, or notes you are jotting down to craft a new resume. In either case, look over that information and document what you see. If you consider yourself to be a seasoned salesperson, does your resume read as such? Does it contain phrases that describe you as a top-notch experienced salesperson or does it blur lines because you have held many jobs? Does it contain language to support your contributions, your achievements, and your results? Do you see phrases such as "proven track record", "outstanding success in", "top-producing" or "ranked top in"? Of course, there can be many more phrases to use, but you get the point. The entire resume should be a story of your professional career with quantifiable, supporting evidence to demonstrate you are the perfect person for the job in which you are applying. Anyone who reads your resume will have no doubt that you are a professional in your field with the skills, abilities, and track record for continued success. Easy story to tell, right? If you are not quite convinced yet, no worries; in this section of the book, we are focusing on your message. To know your message, you need to start documenting your story. It doesn't have to be perfect yet; this is the beginning. It is like molding clay, and I promise you will have more than an unrecognizable lump when you are done. Look to the plan of action for guidance on how to move forward.

In the next chapter, we are going to talk about personal branding and why it is important. We will then follow with naming your audience. Finally, we will move on to the actual resume building.

KEY POINTS OF REFERENCE:

- Everyone has a story, but no one has your story
- Tell your story with confidence
- Do not fudge the truth on your resume

PLAN OF ACTION:

- Gather your story facts, *i.e.* review your resume or your notes about every job you have held. Does it tell your career story the way you want it to? Don't worry about formatting, just look at the words. If it does great, you can put your notes to the side in preparation for the actual resume building. If it does not, what is missing?
- If the words on the page are not conveying your story, or if you are just getting started with a blank page, that is okay. Simply jot down 10 words, in no particular order that you believe describes your career expertise in the way of skills or competencies. Perhaps you would say that you are skilled in budget, finance, project management, or training. After you have finished and are pleased with the words you selected, put your list to the side to use later when you build your resume.

WORDS OF WISDOM:

Do not fudge facts. As Charles Spurgeon so eloquently stated, "A lie can travel halfway around the world while the truth is putting on its shoes."

In other words, that small white lie can turn into a really big one before you know it. It is not worth it, friends.

2

BUILDING YOUR BRAND

This chapter is about building your brand so you can convey your message in a way that resonates consistently and effectively with anyone you come in contact with, *i.e.*, a potential employer, coworker, new people you meet, or even family and friends.

You may be wondering what is so special about building a personal brand. Perhaps you are thinking that this wasn't important the last time you created a resume. Times have changed, my friend. Today, standing out to get the job you desire takes extra effort. Before I jump into the reasons why it is important to build your brand and how to go about it, let me share some information to help you understand it.

Personal branding is no different than product branding for a company. Branding, in a nutshell, is to get someone to pick one product over another product. Classic examples can be seen in toothpaste, soft drinks or clothing. Why do you pick a name brand product over a generic one? Or, one product over another product? As a professor who has taught marketing and as a consumer who has some favorite brands, I can tell you a good brand will do the following:

- Clearly deliver a message that resonates with the intended target audience
- Emotionally connect with that target audience
- Motivate that target audience to make the purchase
- Turn those individuals into loyal customers

How do companies do it? Companies that do it well know that five key factors play a huge role in making or breaking a brand. Trust, connection, credibility, confidence, and authenticity. If consumers feel they can't trust the company, they won't buy any products from it. To build that trust, companies have to connect with their consumers.

They connect by being present in places where their audience can be found. Hence the reason there are advertisements on television, radio, the Internet, and in stores. To be credible, companies, especially new ones, will tie themselves to individuals or companies who have already gained credibility with their intended consumers. They build off the credibility those entities have already built. An example can be seen in companies that connect to actors, singers, and athletes. To build consumer confidence, they need to demonstrate that they offer quality products by finding ways to highlight their expertise. Going back to the toothpaste example, companies connect with dentists who state their toothpaste is better than their competitors. Finally, they must be authentic. The consumer wants to know they care. To demonstrate they care, companies may partner with community service organizations or donate part of their profits to worthy causes.

In today's job market, you need to see yourself as a brand if you want to be taken seriously. Building a personal brand is about those same five key factors mentioned for a company. If you want to get the job you desire, you must build trust, connect with others, have credibility, exude confidence, and be authentic.

Creating Your Personal Brand:

The first question I always get is, how do you do it? Creating a personal brand starts with your words and your actions.

To deliver a message that resonates with a potential employer (or anyone else for that matter), you have to know yourself. This calls for some self-reflection and deep thinking. To know yourself, you need to think about what you value, why you do the things you do, and what motivates you. If you can't figure those things out, how will you be able to connect with or motivate others?

A good way to start is to think through life's stories. In doing so, you can often pinpoint impactful moments that may have transformed you into the person you are today. Did anything happen when you were younger that changed how you view life? Maybe it was a moment when someone gave you great advice that you are still reaping the rewards from today. The key is to write down some moments in time that were transformational. After you have exhausted your thoughts on the matter, review your list and see if any common themes fall out.

Let me give you an example from my life. I grew up in an abusive home and I experienced a lot of brokenness as a result. However, over the years I discovered that brokenness did not have to be the end of my story. I had great mentors along the way and found strength through my faith that guided me to be the person I am today. As a result, I wanted to help others too, which is how I eventually ended up becoming an author, a college professor, a management consultant and now an entrepreneur focused on career coaching. Incidentally, you can read my full story in *Broken to Beautiful: Brokenness is Not the End of Your Story*, available on Amazon and other bookstores.

Back to your themes, what did you determine about yourself? Did you find you wanted to help others too? If not, that is okay. What did you find? Once you figure out what it is for you, the next step is learning how to convey that message while getting people to trust you and what you say. A good way to do that is by creating a one sentence purpose statement.

A purpose statement is a quick way to tell people why you do what you do. It is the easiest way to convey the message and build trust.

A person once asked me, "Jeannine what makes you get out of bed in the morning to do the work you do?" Someone around me jokingly said, "money." No doubt, I like to have money, but no money is not the drive for me. If it were, I would not have left a prominent position where I was making a large salary to start over and grow my small business from the ground up. In fact, I would have quit and gone back to working for someone else if money was my drive. There is a much bigger reason: I do it because I feel called to a greater purpose. Remember, I stated previously I wanted to help others. My purpose statement holds true in everything I do, whether business-focused or family-related: "To be a light for others so they can find their way."

You may wonder why you need to build trust. No matter what you do in life, at some point you will work with people, which requires trust. Relationships are valuable. Relationships are no different in the business world: you get where you are going by having those special professional relationships. Perhaps, as I mentioned in my case, it is a relationship with another person. A mentor, a leader, a co-worker, or a colleague who helps you get to that place you want to be.

Personal branding starts with **trust**. If people trust you, doors will open up to a variety of professional opportunities, i.e., a new job, a speaking engagement, or industry recognition.

The second part of personal branding has to do

with **connection**. Building connections is also an important part of building your brand. To build a brand, you have to get outside of your comfort zone and network with people through events, project work, and mentorship opportunities. I also recommend connecting with common groups outside of your field. Why? This allows you to cast a wider net and reach people you would not normally encounter. Not only are you meeting new people who can help you see things from a different perspective, but you can also build strategic alliances to gain exposure in other areas. Everyone knows someone, and your new contact may have a connection with a person who has an available job in your field.

The third part of personal branding is about **credibility**. A solid reputation for being an expert in an area, doesn't happen overnight. It takes work. To build credibility you can start by reaching out to people you have connected with to help you establish yourself as a thought leader and expert in your field. If you can be seen as a credible person, you will continue to gain recognition in your area of expertise, which will be helpful when the time comes to search for a new position.

The fourth part of personal branding has to do with gaining **confidence**. Well done personal branding will emphasize the strengths of an individual and can give direction as to where to use those strengths. It can also boost an individual's confidence when they know they have something to offer. If you are lacking in confidence, work toward gaining some. Here are some ways to do so. Jot down the things you do well, the awards you have received, and anything else that you feel proud you did. Keep that list handy so that you can continually see it. Sometimes confidence has to do with being reminded of our successes—especially if you have been in a work environment where you dealt with a toxic boss.

The final part to personal branding is all about being **authentic**. Be you! You are made up of more than just your passion, skills, goals, and values. In the job search seek out positions that align to your interests. If you are true to yourself, you will experience fulfillment and meaning.

Resume and Personal Branding:

As you have probably gathered, personal branding goes beyond just the resume; however, you can use the resume as an important tool in your personal branding efforts.

A good way to do that is to note that purpose statement on your resume. The best location for the purpose statement is after your resume headline. We will talk more about resume content in Chapters 5 and 8. For now, focus your attention on the plan of action item at the end of this chapter which is about developing your purpose statement.

KEY POINTS OF REFERENCE:

- Personal Branding requires Trust, Connection, Credibility, Confidence and Authenticity
- Creating a personal purpose statement is something you can share with others that can open the door to getting to know you

PLAN OF ACTION:

- Draft your purpose statement from your list of thoughts where common themes were found

WORDS OF WISDOM:

Ernest Hemingway said, "The best way to find out if you can trust somebody is to trust them."

In the case of branding, people just need to know a little bit about you so they can trust you fully. After that they just need to decide if they want to or not. Most people will trust you unless you give them a reason not to trust you. When people trust you, the other items fall in place, and then you have people in your corner who want you to succeed.

3

NAMING YOUR AUDIENCE

You have been thinking through your core message, story, and purpose statement. You are getting more confident about what you would like to convey, so now you need to understand who you are trying to reach. As you draft your resume, who are you trying to communicate with?

As a strategic communication specialist for the U.S. Navy, one of my jobs was to draft talking points for key leader engagements. To do a good job, I had to know who my audience was, their background, why they were coming, what they wanted to discuss, who were they going to talk to, how long the meeting was, and many other things. I had to know every little detail to prepare my leadership to be successful.

It is no different when it comes to writing a resume. You have to write the resume for the audience, not for yourself. Later in the book, I will walk you step-by-step through the resume writing process. I will teach you everything I know from content to fonts to color to formatting. For now, think about who your potential employer could be. Why? If you know who you are writing your resume for, you will know what to say and how to design it.

What most people do not realize is writing a resume is not a one size fits all for every industry. A resume should be tailored to the prospective employer. Why? Because not all employers are the same.

For example, you have two individuals looking for a job at the same time: one is a lawyer and one is a graphic designer.

A resume for the lawyer would be more traditional in appearance and contain wording that would demonstrate expertise in diction, especially since written and oral communication is how lawyers make their living. A graphic designer's resume would be very different. It would be more modern in appearance; flair, design experience, and applications would outweigh specific word choices and grade point average.

Do you see the difference? *Note:* I will discuss the difference between a traditional and a modern resume in Chapter 8.

Company Reviews:

To determine your audience, think about the types of jobs you would like to explore. If you like project management and plan to seek positions in certain industries, then you will need to research those industries. Start by searching for some common company names online and then go to their websites. How does their site feel? Is it a more traditional site using a color palette consisting mainly of black, grey or navy blue, or is it more of a contemporary site with bright, loud colors that grab your attention? Next, look at the message being conveyed on their sites. What words do they use? What is important to them? What information do they continually push? Do they talk a lot about company culture, diversity, leadership, ethics, or do they focus on other things like social responsibility and giving back? Finally, look for company leadership and other information. Sometimes they will have biographies posted, and communication in the form of press releases, or talking points from speaking engagements.

The review of each site for the industries of interest will provide you with a plethora of information that will also help you decide if you should create a traditional resume or a modern resume for a particular job. I typically create two resumes for my clients, one of each type for that very reason. In the project management example, many companies require this expertise, but a project manager for a television station would be very different than a project manager for a government agency.

Beyond websites, another way to find out about an organization within a particular industry is to visit them. You can do this by setting up informal meetings. You can reach out to those companies of interest, even if they are not hiring, to see if you can stop in to learn more about what they do. Most reputable organizations will be happy to set up a short face-to-face meeting with a representative. They want to present a positive image to the public. Usually, if a face-to-face meeting is not possible, they will offer a quick 15-20 minute phone call to chat. In either case, you will be provided with an opportunity to learn more about the organization directly from someone who works there.

The best way to set up an informal meeting is to

go through someone you know who already works there; however, if you do not know any employees then call the company directly. The organization's phone number can usually be found on their website. The main operator can direct you to the person who can make things happen.

KEY POINTS OF REFERENCE:

- It is important to get to know your audience by conducting a little research on your companies of interest or by chatting with those contacts who work there.
- Determining your audience will go a long way in ensuring you design a resume that fits the reader. To spend all of your time in part two of this book creating a top-notch resume that does not fit your audience will result in a heartbreaking rejection.

PLAN OF ACTION:

- Research companies in different

industries that would offer a position of interest. The goal is to learn more about the company so that you know how to market yourself to the management.

WORDS OF WISDOM:

If you know whom you are connecting with, you will reach them every time.

II

YOUR STORY

4

DON'T BE BORING

You have decided to pursue a new job. You are ready to explore fresh opportunities and deep down you hope this next job will be the one—the dream job with that great company. Friends have shared companies for you to check out, so you start your search there to find that perfect professional fit.

You quickly discover there is a difference between how organizations want to be perceived. Some companies have spent thousands of dollars on branding. They catch your attention with their online visual presence, memorable color scheme, well-designed logos, and catchy tag lines. You are drawn in by what those organizations have to offer.

The other organizations you find seem to care

little for their online presence or the message they share with the world. They have a basic site, containing broken links and site navigation issues. The little information provided does not give you enough to determine if they would be a good company for you. Overall, you are not impressed.

You have completed your research and are ready to pull out the old resume. It has been several years since you needed it, and quite honestly, it needed work when you put it away last time. You know you have your work cut out for you.

After some searching, you find your old resume. Poor thing has been on life support waiting for this moment in time when you would revive it. In looking at your resume you find that it needs a lot of life breathed into it.

You know that resumes have changed over the years, but you are not sure how much. You glance over your resume and find it to be boring, dry, and even lifeless.

If you want to capture the attention of those organizations who spent the money on their brand, and their image then you will need to up your game when it comes to your resume. To do so, you have to think differently.

For instance, who will receive your resume? Recruiters? Human Resources professionals?

Someone else? Remember from Part I of this book, you must know your audience.

Have you ever reviewed someone's resume that was dull and boring? If not in the workplace, how about a coworker's or friend's resume. I am sure you were polite and even offered suggestions but at the end of the day, you probably wanted to gouge your eyes out. Who wants to read boring stuff? Imagine how many resumes a reviewer goes through in a day. The number is staggering. You may be surprised to learn that an organization may receive more than 250 resumes per open position. Since the number has become so great, many companies have started capping the number of applications they accept. For instance, for federal government positions, a posting may state, "first 50 resumes no matter the deadline."

You do not want to be the person who sends another dull resume for the reviewer to sift through. You want to be the person that makes the reviewer want to read the resume.

One way to be that person is to know who your audience is and gear your resume to them, not you! You are applying to fulfill a job they have, not one you already have. Here's another way to think about it: real estate agents will tell sellers to take down all personal pictures in the house. Do you know why? Because the real estate professional wants buyers to picture themselves living in the house, not you and your family there.

It is the same concept for a job. A reviewer wants to know that you will be a good fit for their company, not how awesome you were for their competitor. You will need to discuss your role with the other company, but the key will be to focus clearly and succinctly on defining the scope, challenges, and opportunities for each position. Your selected contributions should showcase your true skills and expertise.

In addition to providing the information the reviewer seeks, you also want your resume to be visually appealing, so you should care a bit about design as well. Just as you care about the first impression you make in the job search; the resume is the first impression that a reviewer will have of you and your brand. If your resume is high quality containing a wealth of information and is beautifully designed, the reviewer will want to call you in for an interview. However, if your resume is boring and lacks visual appeal, you will blend in with the other resumes and then risk falling to the luck of the draw.

A badly designed resume gives your reviewer the impression that you don't care about the organization or the position for which you are applying. Once they form a negative impression of you, it will be hard for you to get an interview.

KEY POINTS OF REFERENCE:

To breathe life into your resume, it must be geared towards the audience and contain information those individuals want to see. Your resume needs to be both informative and visually appealing if you are to make a good impression with a prospective employer. Just as a company spends thousands of dollars on their branding, you need to spend time ensuring your brand comes through effectively on your resume. To be successful, you must:

- Design your resume with the organization in mind
- Create a visually appealing and informative resume
- Make sure your job descriptions define the scope, challenges, and opportunities so that your selected contributions showcase your true skills and expertise

PLAN OF ACTION:

- Pull out every job you have held for the past 10-15 years and determine the scope, challenges, and opportunities for your position. Questions to help you think through this action item: What was the company's overall mission? How did you contribute to the company mission? What was your specific role and what challenges did you encounter in that role? How did you overcome challenges to contribute successfully to the mission? Make sure you capture those details and save them so they are available when it comes time to write your resume.

WORDS OF WISDOM:

Just as Walt Disney said, "You don't build it for yourself. You know what the people want and you build it for them." It is the same concept for the resume. You are not building it for you; you are building it for the reviewer.

5

SIX SECONDS TO
SELL YOURSELF

Today's job search requires a much different approach than from year's past. Just as technology has changed the way we work and live, so has the way we receive information.

In the past, you had to create a resume to be read by a reviewer in hard copy form. Today, most reviewers look at resumes on devices: desktop computers, laptops, mobiles, or even tablets. Gone are the days where a hard copy resume was required.

Don't get me wrong—it is still good practice to print out a couple of resumes to have with you to pass out during an interview if need be, but nowadays, you are designing your resume to be read on-screen.

In the first chapter of this section, I talk about breathing new life into your old resume—do not be boring! I gave you some action items to complete and now, I am going to share what every potential employer expects you to know. They expect you to know what content to include in your resume, how it should be formatted, and what it should look like to meet their approval.

Do not look like a resume rookie. Start by selecting the right resume format. There is a lot of competition when seeking a position and not everyone knows what resume format is appropriate for both the level of the position sought and the profession or industry in which the job exists.

Format - Types:

Start by putting the resume in an appropriate format. Three main types of resume formats have been popular over the years. The **chronological, functional** (also referred to as a skills-based resume), and the **combination**.

Chronological means your resume reads in order (*i.e.*, linear, consecutive, sequential). In the case of a chronological resume, the job experience, education, and other activities are all listed in descending date order with the most recent items appearing at the top.

This is the preferred format by employers. Why? Because it is the most common resume type and thus, the most recognizable. Employers like to use this type because it is also easy to catch gaps on a resume.

A **functional** resume highlights several key areas of experience, responsibilities, and accomplishments. This is a good one to use if you are seeking a new job in an area that you have not worked in for many years. You can easily pull that old experience up to highlight it without confusing the reviewer with dates.

In this type of resume, you would use a lot of description and context following each section to highlight and provide supporting evidence for your strengths.

Functional resumes in the modern job market are typically used for high school and college graduates with minimal professional experience.

A **combination** resume is just as it sounds: a combination of the chronological and functional resume. It covers both worlds by grouping relevant skills into a chronological format from most recent to oldest job positions. On this resume all information is relevant.

Sample resumes for all three types can be found here:

http://bit.ly/breatheresume

Now that you know what format is most popular, let's talk about what needs to be included in a resume.

Content - 3 by 3 Format:

An effective resume needs to showcase several key items. First and foremost, list your name, address (city and state only), phone number, and email address at the top of the page. Some people include their LinkedIn URL, and that is okay as well. The information must be visible and easy to decipher so the potential employer will know how to reach you.

After the heading information is complete, I always make sure there is enough information conveyed for the reviewer to determine that my client is the most qualified person for the job. To do this, I start with what I call my "3 by 3 format." The first three items are the front matter and appear at the top of the resume after your heading.

1. Headline
2. Summary
3. Core Skills

The second three items follow and include:

1. Experience
2. Education
3. Other

Note: If you are a new graduate with little experience, you can (and should) put education before experience. Again, this is only for recent graduates with little work experience.

The 3 by 3 "other" category includes items such as professional recognition, publications, speaking engagements, community affiliations, or volunteer service.

It depends on the client, the type of job they are seeking, the industry they are applying in, and the story the client needs to present.

I am telling you to start with the front matter because you have 6 seconds to sell yourself to the person reviewing your resume. If they are not impressed immediately, you lose out on the opportunity for them to continue reading any further down in your resume.

Layout:

When most people think about layout, magazines and newspapers come to mind. A good magazine or newspaper has a well-ordered arrangement and subscribers know where to look for the information every time they view the publication. The layout of the publication always contains certain items of interest to keep the subscriber engaged. This is no different for a resume. Your goal in writing your resume is to engage the potential employer. You need to post the information in a way they are accustomed to seeing it. If you stray too much, you make them work—and they won't search long for that information. They will move on to the next resume.

Bottom line, the resume should be easy to read and decipher. Use the 3 by 3 format: headline, summary and core skills at the top, followed by professional experience noted into roles in chronological order, with the top three accomplishments followed by educational qualifications, and any other items relevant to the role. This allows potential employers to do a quick read before an interview to size up the candidate. The other information can be reviewed later as part of their deeper review.

Resume Length:

I often get asked how long a resume really should be. A resume should be short and concise. For a recent high school or college graduate, one page (front side only) is sufficient. For a person with up to 10 years of experience, you should be able to comfortably include all information on one page, front, and back.

For a person with significant experience, you can do two pages, front and back of the paper. However, it is important to note that the reviewer wants to know the details about only the most recent 7 - 10 years. After that point, the information is considered dated.

Resume – Curriculum Vitae (CV):

I would be remiss if I did not mention two other types of resumes: the curriculum vitae (CV) and the federal job resume (USAJOBS.gov).

The CV is typically used in the world of academia by postgraduate students seeking scholarly, research, or grant-type positions. In this case, they need to document all life achievements to appeal to their audience. There is no true set number of pages for a CV. My CV, which has landed me several teaching positions with different universities over the years, is seven pages long. I have friends who are tenured professors with CVs that are 20 pages long thanks to the many scholarly publications they have written.

CVs are often the communication medium of choice for foreign countries as well. Most recently, I drafted a CV for an Australian client who worked in Europe and several other countries over the years. I also crafted a resume for the same individual for a non-profit position here in the states. If you are applying to a company outside of the United States be sure to check the job listing to make certain you understand what type of document you need to submit, a resume or a CV.

Resume – Federal Government (USAJOBS) Resume:

A federal government resume is also one that can be longer. The reason stems from the amount of information required to convey on the document. If you are applying for a federal job, you must list the following for every job you have held for the past 10 years.

- Organization
- Location/Address
- Start and End Dates
- Your Job Title
- Full-time or Part-time Status
- Number of Hours Worked
- Salary (annually or hourly)
- Supervisor's First and Last Names, Phone Number, and if the reviewer can contact them ("May contact" or "Contact me first").

Due to the additional information, it is common for a federal resume to be between three and seven pages long (front and back of the page). Yes, you read that right.

KEY POINTS OF REFERENCE:

In this chapter, you learned the things employers expect you to know and how to capture their attention quickly.

- Use the proper resume format (chronological, functional/skills-based, combination)
- Include a contact header that contains your name, address (city and state only), phone number, email, and LinkedIn URL, if you have one
- Use my 3 by 3 format to remember what to include: Headline, Summary, Core Skills, Experience, Education, Other. Other items include professional recognition, publications, speaking engagements, community affiliations or volunteer service
- Keep your resume, short and concise. Resume length is between 1 and 2 pages
- CVs and Federal Government Resumes are longer

PLAN OF ACTION:

- Determine the type of resume you need to create
- Jot down your header information so you have it handy
- Pull out the list of every job you have

held from last chapter's action item so it is easily accessible when you begin building the resume

WORDS OF WISDOM:

Educating yourself with things you are expected to know will give you a leg up against your competition.

6

BUILDING THE FOUNDATION

Building the foundation of the resume goes a bit deeper than knowing format type, content, and layout. In this chapter, we are going to focus on some best practices for formatting, readability, and fonts.

Since this book is for anyone who needs to write a resume no matter the age, it is important to address some best practices for good formatting upfront.

Best Practice 1 - Spacing after punctuation

There is only one (1) space after punctuation. If you are like me, this one is tough. I grew up with typewriters, not computers. On the typewriter, we had to space twice after punctuation to ensure there was enough space between sentences. With the prominence of computers and the plethora of fonts, that issue no longer exists, so the need for extra spacing is also gone.

Best Practice 2 - Tab functionality

This one is also like the previous best practice. In the days of the typewriter, we had limited tab setting capability, so when we couldn't adjust our tabs on a manual typewriter, we would space in five times for our indent. Computers have opened the door to tabbing functionality, so we no longer have to use the space bar. You can simply set your tab marks using the word processing application of choice. No matter the application, you can go into your software's help or support area and type in the word **tab** and instructions should come up to guide you through the process.

The key to this best practice is to make certain you are no longer using the space bar to adjust items on your resume. If you do, the reviewer on the other end may not have his or her settings adjusted the same way, and this can cause your resume to look odd. Be safe and set tabs so that your resume won't have formatting issues for the reviewer.

Best Practice 3 - Consistency

It is important to be consistent in your resume. If in the experience section, you put the organization in all caps but bold your role title, then do that for every entry. The same goes for the order of entries. If in your experience section, you note organization first, then role title, you should follow suit for the education and other sections as well. For instance, in the education section, put the school in all caps and bold the degree.

Resume reviewers do a consistency check to see if you pay attention to details. If you note in your core skills area that you are detail-oriented and then are not consistent, you will lose points with the reviewer.

Best Practice 4 - Proofread

I can't stress this enough. If you have an error on your resume, you probably won't get the job. The reviewer is looking for someone who pays attention to details and can be counted on to produce quality work. If you produce a resume littered with errors, you will not impress the reviewer.

I highly recommend you have someone else review your resume for errors. Our brains tend to see what we want to see and thus miss glaring errors. If you do not have someone who can read the resume for you then use your read-aloud application under the review tab in Microsoft Word. Other word processing applications may have this feature as well. You can use the help or support feature to find out if your program uses it or something similar.

In turning on the read-aloud feature, the resume will be read back to you. I use this feature when I do client work to help me catch errors that I may have missed.

Best Practice 5 - Readability

In person, we all know first impressions are important. It is the same with a resume. During a review, you get 6 seconds to make a good first impression with your resume, so make it count.

Use bullets, sub-bullets, and columns when appropriate to quickly showcase your skills. Too much text makes it hard for the reader to find what is important.

Best Practice 6 - Fonts

Two main factors that influence which font you should select: space considerations and appearance. It is best to use fonts that are universally accepted by all users. In other words, most word processing programs will contain common fonts, so you don't need to be concerned that your resume will change in appearance if the reviewer doesn't have that particular font. There are also two different font typefaces: Serif and Sans Serif.

Serif fonts are those where curves are added to the ends of the letters. Sans is merely a French word meaning without so Sans Serif means without those added curves on the letters.

Serif – see the curves at the end of the letters.

Sans Serif – see no curves at the ends of the letters.

Figure 1. Serif and Sans Serif

The most common fonts are shown on the next page.

Serifs:

- Book Antiqua
- Bookman Old Style
- Cambria
- Garamond
- Georgia
- Palatino Linotype
- Times New Roman

Sans Serifs:

- Arial, **Arial Black**, Arial Narrow
- Calibri
- **Impact**
- Lucida Sans
- Tahoma
- Verdana

Note: all fonts are size 12. Notice the difference in size and spacing. Both something to consider when determining your font choice for your resume. Remember, the overall appearance of your resume and what it communicates will be at stake so choose wisely.

Here is a closer view of what font sizing can do to text in a resume:

All 12-point fonts: San Serifs

Calibri, Calibri, Calibri, Calibri, Calibri, Calibri, Calibri
Arial, Arial, Arial, Arial, Arial, Arial, Arial, Arial
Verdana, Verdana, Verdana, Verdana

All 12-point fonts: Serifs
Garamond, Garamond, Garamond, Garamond
Book Antiqua, Book Antiqua, Book Antiqua
Cambria, Cambria, Cambria, Cambria, Cambria

Figure 2. Font Size Comparison

All 9-point fonts: San Serifs

Calibri, Calibri, Calibri, Calibri, Calibri, Calibri, Calibri, Calibri
Arial, Arial, Arial, Arial, Arial, Arial, Arial, Arial, Arial
Verdana, Verdana, Verdana, Verdana, Verdana

All 9-point fonts: Serifs

Garamond, Garamond, Garamond, Garamond, Garamond
Book Antiqua, Book Antiqua, Book Antiqua
Cambria, Cambria, Cambria, Cambria, Cambria, Cambria

Figure 3. Small Font Size Comparison

Choose the best font and font size for your resume. To determine which font and font size is best, ask these questions: Which font can be read the easiest in the smallest size should you need to shrink text to fit more items? Which font is not over-bearing when increased?

My recommendation is to stay with an 11 or 12 point size for fonts that are serifs and a 10 or 11 point size for fonts that are sans serif.

The point is to create a resume that can be easily read by both a system and a human. Do not use your favorite font if it happens to be an common font.

Note: Applicant Tracking Systems are not coded for non-universal fonts so your resume will get kicked out of the system never to be seen by the person doing the hiring if you use them. Hence, my advice is don't risk it!

Best Practice 7: Online Search

Make your resume readable for the human eye and the computer. The best way to do that is to stick with common fonts that are classified as Sans Serif. Again, those fonts without the wings. Arial, Calibri, Tahoma, and Verdana are some of my favorites.

Most online job postings require you to upload your resume into a system that goes to the company. It may then also be fed into another company applicant tracking system.

KEY POINTS OF REFERENCE:

There are seven best practice (BP) tips focused on formatting, readability, and fonts

- BP 1: Spacing after punctuation (one space, not two)
- BP 2: Tab functionality
- BP 3: Consistency
- BP 4: Proofread
- BP 5: Readability
- BP 6: Fonts
- BP 7: Online Search

PLAN OF ACTION:

- Review the common fonts shared and determine which would be best to use based on the information you pulled in previous chapters, *i.e.*, job, education, etc.

WORDS OF WISDOM:

Make a good first impression on paper and in person!

7

GOOD DESIGN GOES
A LONG WAY

In this chapter, the focus is on visual appeal, good design and color usage.

Visual Appeal:

Just as songs have hooks to capture the attention of the listener, you must use tactics to help you stand out from the competition to capture the attention of the reviewer. The tactics in the case of the resume can be lines, borders, boxes, images, graphics, and illustrations. In every case, the goal is to create a visually appealing resume to attract attention.

In Word, you can easily add lines, borders, and boxes by using the Border Feature found under the

Paragraph section in the main ribbon at the top of the software program. Here are basic instructions to help you out.

Select a word, line or paragraph then go to Home > Borders

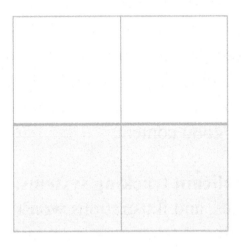

Figure 4. Microsoft Borders Graphic

and then open the menu of border choices. Choose the type of border you want. If you have never used the Border Feature before then I recommend you use the Help area at the top of the ribbon to search for borders. A sidebar of options will open on the right side of your computer screen and there you will see the option for text borders with an easy to use step-by-step process to walk you through the procedure.

With regards to images, graphics, and illustrations, you can add them; however, I do not recommend them for every industry for a couple of reasons:

Reason 1: You don't need to. A resume is still not the place to include a personal picture. You do not need to add your profile picture because a prospective employer will look you up on LinkedIn. They can see your profile picture there, so save your resume space for good content.

Reason 2: Applicant tracking systems. Adding images, graphics, and illustrations won't make it through an applicant tracking system, and you won't be informed. You will be waiting to hear from the job you think you applied to but will never get word because you never truly applied.

Is there ever a time to add images, graphics, and illustrations? Yes, especially if you are working or seeking to work in a field where graphic design, web design, and other creative talents are required. Given the field and the application process, an applicant tracking system isn't typically used. Instead, creatives will use electronic portfolio-type sites in many cases to share their resume along with samples of their work to impress the reviewer.

Adding lines, borders, boxes, images, graphics, and illustrations are attractive, distinctive, and, can help you stand out from the competition. Don't use images, graphics, or illustrations unless you are applying for a job that requires them as mentioned previously.

Design Considerations:

To make your resume as visually appealing as possible you have to use all tactics at your disposal.

Tactic 1: Page Balance

Page balance is about making sure there is not so much text on a page that the words run together or is too difficult to read. A good way to think about this is to recall a book you may have read that was filled with a lot of information but no pictures. The smaller the book and the greater the information, results in more eye strain. Eventually, the reader will be forced to stop reading. The same is true for a person who has to read hundreds of resumes at a sitting. After a while, the overbearing text on a page causes the reviewer to give up and toss the resume.

A good rule of thumb is to have good page margins so you do not try to cram too much text on the page. My recommendation is to not go smaller than .7 or bigger than 1 inch for your margins. Some people say you can go as small as .5 but I caution you, many printers will cut off the page if the margins are that small. My advice is to not risk going too small.

Tactic 2: Focus

The point of a resume is to entice a reviewer enough to call you in for an interview. Upfront, visual appeal is the focus. In Chapter 5, you learned that your contact information should appear first followed by a prominent headline. Why? Your name immediately personalizes your resume and your headline instantly tells the reviewer what you specialize in. Chapter 7 provides examples of how to highlight your contact information and your headline so you can grab the reader's attention.

A purpose statement can be included at this point. The purpose statement (or, as I like to call it, the branding statement) should go below the headline but before the summary area we discussed in earlier chapters. As mentioned previously a purpose statement is a good way to provide positive and purpose-driven information for the reviewer. You may recall my purpose statement shared in Chapter 2: "To be a light for others so they can find their way."

Tactic 3: Text Appearance

How does your text appear on the page? Are those things you are trying to highlight standing out or getting lost in the sea of words. In Chapter 6, you saw font size does make a difference. There are other ways to draw attention to words too. If you want to emphasize something, try using larger fonts. This would be good for your name, headline, and section headers. If you want to catch the reader's eye quickly then using bolder fonts will do the trick. Finally, if you want to really get noticed than go with reverse text for contrast to give you that pop.

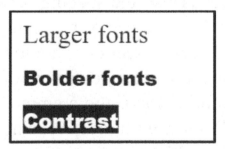

Figure 5. Text Appearance

Tactic 4: White Space

White Space is basically as it sounds, the white you see on the page. This goes back to the discussion we just had on readability. You need to make sure there is enough white space so that the reader won't miss words or experience eye strain. On the flip side, you do not want too much white space either as that could cause the text to look odd. Use white space to your advantage to change the way the text looks. Below are examples of condensing text to make it fit as well as expanding text to make it take up more room. Neither is good as shown.

Here is an example of not enough white space.

Here is an example of too much white space.

Figure 6. Spacing

White space is also the spacing between items on the resume. For instance, subheadings, bulleted text items, and resume sections should have adequate spacing to allow for a good flow of information. If the information is too crammed together the reader will not want to keep reading. Allow for good separations. If the text won't fit, then you have too much text on your resume.

Tactic 5: Consistency

Consistency is vital. Resume reviewers do a consistency check to see if you are detail-oriented. Consistency is about following through on the overall design. For instance, if you put a period at the end of a bulleted sentence, then do it for all bulleted sentences. I prefer not to use periods at the end of bullets because they are not full sentences, but you can as long as you are consistent. The same goes for other features you choose to use, such as bold and italics. If you bold the organization in the job listing, then do it for all your job listings. If you note the name of the organization first then your role title, be consistent and do it for all job listings on your resume.

Tactic 6: Color

Color is no longer taboo. In the modern job search, color is important to help you stand out from the competition. I recommend the color navy blue because the color suggests trust. You can use other colors, such as green, red, or brown, but be aware that colors evoke a response. For instance, did you know that green is used as a calming color? Red typically conjures up hunger, which is why many restaurants include red and orange in their color scheme. Red is also considered a power color, so if you use it too much, you may aggravate the reviewer. Finally, as I mentioned, blue, which is my preference, evokes trust but it is also a confident color. I recommend color for your name, headlines, and other resume section headings. The key is to use color sparingly as a nice touch, not overbearingly where the resume is completely a color other than the standard black. Too much of a good thing will ruin the effect. For instance, if everything is bold and blue, nothing stands out so it defeats your efforts of adding elements to catch the reader's attention. Less is more on the resume.

KEY POINTS OF REFERENCE:

The point of this chapter was to learn about creating a visually appealing resume to capture the attention of the reader, implementing good design, and using colors effectively.

Good design requires many elements: having a point of focus, appropriate page balance, allotted white space, and required consistency. Design is geared towards attracting and keeping the attention of the reader as well as sharing important information.

PLAN OF ACTION:

If you are not familiar with the tools in Microsoft Word, I recommend you do some Word tutorials so that you can create a more dynamic resume. You can find great tutorials on YouTube, Microsoft Office, and LinkedIn Learning.

Note: The free resources link provided in the Thank You section of this book will also take you to some resume examples and templates you can use.

WORDS OF WISDOM:

As Franklin D. Roosevelt said, "there are many ways of going forward, but only one way of standing still." This quote is especially relevant when it comes to resume writing. If you want to move forward and secure the job of your dreams you have to deploy tactics that will help you stand out from the competition. Don't stand still; keep moving forward toward your goal!

8

STORYBOARDING
YOUR RESUME

Now that you have found your core message, completed your plans of action from each previous chapter, and thought about the information you need to include, it is time to start thinking about putting your story to paper. You can do so by storyboarding your resume just like you would a presentation, paper, report, or any other type of written document.

To help you with your storyboarding, I recommend reviewing the two resumes I have included in the back of this book. You can also see more examples by checking out the additional free resources I have provided. You can gain access to them by going to the Thank You (Free Gift - Bonus Materials) section found toward the back of this book.

The free bonus materials include sample resumes you can review for ideas and actual templates you can use to create your resume.

The first thing to do is note your name, city with state abbreviation, phone number, email address, and LinkedIn URL (if you have one) at the top of your page. Why just city and state abbreviation for your address? A couple of reasons:

1. Today, there are so many faster ways to contact you that no one sends mail anymore.
2. We are very connected these days and people are willing to travel for a position that meets their needs. For instance, you may live in Virginia but work in D.C. Hence, location on the resume does not carry the weight it once did.

As you look at your contact information, how do you think you can help it stand out more?

Figures 7 - 9 provides some good examples.

Sally Sample
Any City, ST
Sally.sample@gmail.com
757-456-7890

Figure 7. Normal Layout Example

SALLY SAMPLE
Any City, ST | 757.456.7890 | sally.sample@gmail.com | www.linkedin.com/in/sally-sample

Figure 8. Enhanced Layout Example

Sally Sample
Any City, ST | 757.456.7890 | sally.sample@gmail.com | www.linkedin.com/in/sally-sample

Figure 9. More Intense Layout Example

Note: Do not put credentials after your name unless you hold a terminal degree, such as a Ph.D. Hence, do not put a CPA, M.B.A., etc. It will make you look like a resume rookie.

Tip: If you have a LinkedIn profile make sure you tailor the URL. Many people forget to do that, and it tells a reviewer you are not tech savvy or knowledgeable with social media platforms. If your LinkedIn URL contains the default numbers at the end of it, you need to tailor it. Here is a link to a blog article I wrote that walks you through the tailoring process step-by-step with illustrations.

http://bit.ly/tailor-url

Once you figure out how you would like your contact information to look, you can then move on to the 3 by 3 format starting with your headline.

Creating a headline quickly tells the reviewer you are an expert in a particular area.

Samples Headlines:

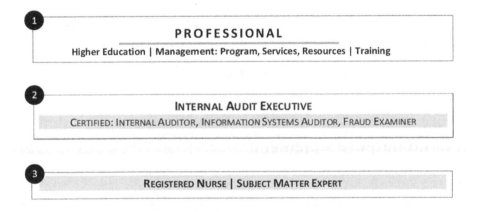

Figure 10. Sample Headlines

Note: Notice that each heading is designed a bit differently. There is no wrong way to design your heading, just make sure the wording used represents who you are and what you are considered to be an expert in.

Once you are pleased with the headline you have created, move on to the summary section of your resume. The summary is not an objective. Resumes no longer use the old objective to tell the reviewer they want a job in a particular area. It is assumed that the person's objective is to get a job so the new format opts for using the space to summarize your expertise. Some call it the Value Proposition area. You can also include your **purpose statement (aka branding statement)** in this section. If you choose to do a **purpose statement,** include it after the heading. Be sure to put a space after the headline and before the statement.

Here is the fourth headline with summary included but no purpose statement:

4

MARKETING | COMMUNICATIONS | GRAPHIC DESIGN | EVENT PLANNING

Award-winning professional dedicated to supporting leadership, teammates and clients. Skilled in marketing, communications, graphic design, and event planning. Proven success as a creative, forward thinker and detailed, organized planner. Possess strong communication skills and ability to motivate others to perform at high levels through training, mentoring, and setting of clear expectations.

Figure 11. Headline with Summary

Note: In the fourth example, the heading with a summary contains 4 lines. I would stick to 3-4 lines max to be memorable by the reader.

You can find a sample resume with a **purpose statement/branding statement** in the bonus materials I discussed previously.

Finally, when you have completed your contact header, your headline, and summary, you are ready to include the core skills area. Core skills are just as they sound: skills listed to convey your expertise. You can post your items in alphabetical order or another logical order, just be sure the logic you use when creating lists is common enough to resonate with the person reviewing it. You want to share with the reviewer quickly your experience and what you are known for in an easy to read list. Do not overcomplicate it.

Here is an example of core skills in a resume:

• Team Leadership & Change Management	• Fundraising & Donor Interactions
• Strategic Planning & Execution	• Creativity & Innovation
• Assessment, Measurement & Outcome Analysis	• Diversity & Internationalization
• Budget, Resource Planning & Execution	• Key Leader Engagement & Partnership Building
• Shared Governance, Communication & Collaboration	• Talent Recruitment, Retention & Institution Growth Management
• Internal & External Relations	• Strategic Communications, Outreach & Public Speaking
• Fiscal, Administrative & Programmatic Oversight	

Figure 12. Core Skills Example

Note: The key skills area should be short. It can be two or three columns and should match the skills called for in the job posting. This example is not in alphabetical order but commonality order.

You have now finished the first 3 of the 3 by 3 format. It is time to look at the second 3, which starts with experience.

Documenting Experience:

There are many ways that you can list your entries. Here are some examples to get you thinking.

If you are short on space you can go with a one-line entry for company, role, location, and dates.

GREAT COMPANY, **Chief Compliance Officer**	Norfolk, VA | 2014 – Present
Or you can switch the organization and title around. You would put the company first if it is a prominent company. You would put the title first if you are trying to highlight the fact that you have held a position like the position you are applying to. No matter what you do, just be consistent with all your entries.	
Chief Compliance Officer, Great Company	Norfolk, VA | 2014 – Present

Figure 13. Documenting Experience Example 1

If you have space to spread out, you can go with a two-line entry as shown in Figure 14.

GREAT COMPANY   Norfolk, VA | 2014 – Present
Chief Compliance Officer

Or

Chief Compliance Officer   Norfolk, VA | 2014 – Present
Great Company

Figure 14. Documenting Experience Example 2

You can also do the entry this way:

GREAT COMPANY, Norfolk, VA 2014 – Present
Chief Compliance Officer

Or

GREAT COMPANY | Chief Compliance Office | Norfolk, VA 2014 – Present

Figure 15. Documenting Experience Example 3

Note: Notice I have used the vertical line (|) several times first in my headlines and now in my experience section. Vertical lines are a great way to highlight information cleanly and professionally. They are good for helping you save space and making things stand out on the page.

No matter which way you decide to convey the information, the key is to be consistent. Choose a format and stick with it throughout the resume.

Now we are ready to add our description to the

experience items. You can do this in several ways. You can add a challenge statement followed by selected contributions. It is important to note that you will not use personal pronouns in your resume. In other words, do not use "I" in your resume bullets.

Instead start with action verbs such as advise, champion, design or influence. There are many action verbs to choose from. A list of action verbs is included in the free bonus materials provided so be sure to check them out.

Figure 16 is an example:

GREAT ORGANIZATION	Norfolk, VA | 2014 – 2018

Chief Compliance Officer

Challenge: Ensuring Great Organization, a publicly traded company, operates in a legal and ethical manner complying with all regulatory requirements while meeting business objectives.

Selected Contributions & Achievements:

- Designed and built best in class compliance management system in less than 5 years. **Result:** System evaluated and approved annually by large money center banks and state and federal regulators

Figure 16. Documenting Experience Example 4

You do not have to include a challenge statement; you could just use a description of what you do and then jump into bullets.

Here's an example of an entry with no challenge statement:

GREAT ORGANIZATION   Norfolk, VA | 2014 – 2018
Chief Compliance Officer

Served as Global Chief Compliance Officer for $908M, publicly traded company with approximately 400 employees. Managed $24M budget.

Selected Contributions & Achievements:

- Designed and built best in class compliance management system in less than 5 years. **Result:** System evaluated and approved annually by large money center banks and state and federal regulators

---

Figure 17. Documenting Experience Example 5

Note: Do not list jobs that are older than 10 years unless you are applying for a federal job. If you have worked with one company for more than 10 years but have held several roles during that time, you can do the following:

GREAT ORGANIZATION   Norfolk, VA | 2014 – 2018
Chief Compliance Officer (2014 – 2018)

Short description of role

Selected Contributions & Achievements:
- Important bullet here

Compliance Officer (2012 – 2014)

Short description of role

Selected Contributions & Achievements:
- Important bullet here

Figure 18. Documenting Experience Example 6

Federal Resume Experience Listing

If you are applying for a federal job, you must list the following for every job through 10 years: organization, address, start and end dates, title, full-time or part-time status, hours worked per week, salary (annually or hourly), supervisor's first and last name, supervisor's phone number, and "may contact" or "contact me first."

Note: If you are military and you have been in 20 or 30 years, you can do the following:

U.S. NAVY (RECENT)   Various Locations| 2009 – 2019

GREAT COMMAND 1 (2016 – 2019)
1234 B Street, Virginia Beach, VA 23462
Chief Compliance Officer, Full-Time, 40 hours per week, $100,000
Supervisor: CAPT Joe Smith, 757.555.4444; may contact

Short description of role
Selected Contributions & Achievements:
•   Important bullet here

GREAT COMMAND 21 (2013 – 2016)
567 A Street, Virginia Beach, VA 23462
Chief Compliance Officer, Full-Time, 40 hours per week, $100,000
Supervisor: CAPT Mary Smith, 757.444.8888; may contact

Short description of role
Selected Contributions & Achievements:
•   Important bullet here

Figure 19. Documenting Experience Example 7

Note: List the most recent positions from 10 years forward.

For positions older than 10 years, create a section in your resume called **"Early Career"** for those entries. The good news is you only need the name of the organization, location (city, state), start and end dates, and job title. You do not need the other information mentioned previously or any descriptions unless you choose to do so. If you do choose to add a few points about the job, do not include more than three bullets.

Now that you know how to list your job description, let's focus on what you should include for those bulleted items.

Content – Crafting your Descriptors/Bullets

As you design your bullets, it is important to remember, **it is about the role, not you**. People tend to spend way too much time talking about their accomplishments, even if it is not related to the role they are applying for.

Here is another way to think of it. A doctor can treat many ailments. He knows about several medicines but is focused on the patient's need then. Does he write a generic prescription, or does he write one that is targeted to the ailment as a resolution to the suffering patient's problem? He writes one for that patient's needs. The resume has to offer a solution to the role—nothing more!

A resume is a marketing document, not an HR toolkit. The resume must highlight your top three (3) accomplishments in every role. You should not need more than three (3).

Bullet points must be specific. Telling someone you have saved costs or increased sales without providing some supporting evidence means nothing. Instead, state that you saved the company $5M with the xyz project implementation or you increased sales by 25% over your tenure in the role.

Let's look at some resume phrases to get you thinking about your options:

- Proven track record of…
- Within ___ period of time…
- Experienced in all facets of…
- Promoted from… to …
- Innovation resulted in…

For specific bullet descriptors, the goal is to again show quantifiable information, a result of some sort. Here are some examples:

- Spearheaded cost reduction and efficiency efforts. **Result:** Despite downturn in revenue, improved bottom line by 25% through implementation of key business strategies
- Guided $1M project geared toward employee satisfaction. **Result:** 50% increase in office morale, customer service, and diversity
- Recruited to bolster lending operation for small bank established in 1986. **Result:** Bank increased membership from 10,000 to 25,000 members in one year and increased bank deposits from $90 million to $125 million

Note: For veterans trying to convert their military jargon into civilian terms, a site I have used often is called O*Net Online and can be found here: https://www.onetonline.org/

In demonstrating that you are a results-oriented individual through the language used in your statements, you are telling the prospective employer that you are indeed worth the money. This is how you get hired and paid what you are worth!

Words to use and not use on your resume:

Do not use dated or overused words. There are better words to use to help your personal story stand out.

Examples of overused words:

- Responsible for
- Accountable for
- Duties included
- Led, managed, organized

The first three on the list are not necessary. Instead of stating you are "responsible for," just note the tasks that you are responsible for.

For example, "responsible for tracking monthly statements" is better stated, "Track monthly statements."

The words in the fourth bullet are very overused. I once had an HR person tell me if she had to review one more resume in which the individual says he led or managed something she would go crazy!

Friends, you must think like a reviewer. Imagine in a stack of 100 resumes how many people state they have led or managed something. I bet every one of them. To stand out and make the money you are worth, you need to demonstrate your true talent, and that includes using words that will impress the reader.

Below are other words to consider. The list is not all-inclusive list. It is meant to get you thinking about words to potentially use.

- Administered
- Advised
- Advocated
- Arbitrated
- Capitalized
- Chaired
- Championed
- Clarified
- Collaborated
- Commissioned
- Composed
- Consulted
- Corresponded
- Delegated
- Eased
- Elevated
- Enhanced
- Established
- Expedited

- Facilitated
- Governed
- Guided
- Headed
- Influenced
- Interfaced
- Maximized
- Motivated
- Negotiated
- Operated
- Orchestrated
- Programmed
- Reconciled
- Redesigned
- Restructured
- Solved
- Spearheaded
- Standardized
- Stimulated
- Unified

Instead of using the word **led**, what word looks better from the list? How about championed, chaired, headed, or spear-headed? Instead of the word **managed**, how about delegated, advised, facilitated, or motivated?

A good tool to use when seeking out word options for your resume is a thesaurus. I know it's not a new idea, but it is still a valid one.

Another tool to use is Google search. Type in synonyms for "led" or any other word you are trying to change up. Several dictionaries will offer various definitions with words in sentence form and with synonyms to use for each appropriate definition.

Yet another tool I like to use is job postings themselves. I do an Internet search on job types I am interested in and review various job descriptions to see which words they are using.

Finally, I like to use social media sources such as LinkedIn to see what language is being used by influencers and individuals I highly respect in my network.

Proper Grammar Usage:

It is important to talk about grammar, specifically for bulleted entries, before we move on. If you are still in the position with the company, all your sentences should start with action verbs in the present tense. If you are no longer with the company, then those same action verbs should be in the past tense. Check out Figure 20 for an example of both types.

Present Tense:

- Design and build best in class management systems

Past Tense:

- Designed and built best in class management systems

Figure 20. Grammar Usage

Final advice for making your bullets stand out:

No matter what type of job you are seeking, you need to make sure the information stands out. The way you phrase your bullet statements is important, especially for transitioning military or career changers. You need to use the language recognized in your field of interest. This goes back to knowing your audience. If you use military jargon for a civilian resume, depending on the job you are applying to, you stand a 50/50 chance of the reviewer knowing what you are talking about, even if they have also spent time in the military.

I experienced this early on in my resume writing career. I had the misperception that having a 10-year career serving the military community meant I would easily be able to translate everything military. Wrong! I had to learn to ask the right questions, inquire about acronyms, and seek guidance when something was not clear. For example, Army and Navy both have the Explosive Ordnance Disposal (EOD) capability but that does not necessarily mean they do the same functions. Having worked with Navy EOD I know EOD technicians go to dive school and are trained to deal with underwater explosives in addition to land hazards. I assumed that Army EOD techs focused their attention solely on land hazards. I was wrong. If Army techs are working in a joint environment, they may indeed work in an underwater capacity with their Navy EOD counterparts. Hence, the crossover does exist. It is imperative to ask the question about true experiences to get it right on paper.

The same is true for you. To make sure your bullet statements resonate with the reviewer requires some homework and creativity. The homework consists of company research. Find a job of interest, look at the language in the job posting, and make note of terms they use. Then go to the company website and read through each page. What stands out to you? What terms do they consistently use? What capabilities do they highlight? Just like you are trying to convey that you are the perfect candidate, the company is trying to tell the world they are the perfect company, so use the language from their site to give back to them. Why? Because it will resonate with them!

Additional supporting evidence to help you get the pay you are worth is your education section. The education section tells the reviewer you are dedicated to acquiring knowledge through formal and informal learning endeavors. You can include education from universities noting your degrees, but you can also call out professional training through outside entities as well. The goal again is to demonstrate that you are a lifelong learner.

Education Section:

Just like experience, there are many ways to design the education section as well.

NATIONAL DEFENSE UNIVERSITY   Washington, DC | 1999
Master of Science: National Security Strategy
•   Distinguished Graduate
Or

NATIONAL DEFENSE UNIVERSITY, M.S. National Security Strategy   Washington, DC | 1999

Or

NATIONAL DEFENSE UNIVERSITY, M.S. National Security Strategy, Washington, DC 1999

Figure 21. Education

As you work through the education section, I must

again stress that you should be consistent throughout your resume. For instance, if your job experience listings have the organization in all caps with no bolding then you should do the same for your college entry or any entry in which you include an organization and some sort of role or other items of importance you are stressing for that organization.

If you are a recent graduate, some things you can do to stand out include relevant courses taken while in school. Do not list every course, just those that align with the job you are seeking. For instance, if you are seeking a position with a company doing project management, then include the courses you have taken that directly relate to project management.

You can also list projects you worked on, clubs you belong to, and any honors or awards you received. After five years of employment you no longer list GPA and relevant courses.

Note: If you are a new graduate, remember to list core skills, then education, then experience.

Other Sections:

The other sections of your resume can include items

such as professional recognition, publications, speaking engagements, community affiliations, or volunteer service. For each section you choose to use, the same rules apply as experience, meaning you should not include items more than 10 years old. The goal of including additional items in your resume is merely to highlight that you can do something. For example, noting 1 publication or 10 publications makes no difference because you have demonstrated the skill of writing when you posted the first one. The same is true for speaking engagements: note a couple but don't get carried away. You want the reviewer to be im-pressed, not bogged down or overwhelmed when reading your resume. You want to include enough information to create a good conversation during an interview.

For each category you include, be consistent. Remember, if you have listed organizations first in your experience section, be sure to do the same for education and other sections too. If you noted the organization entries in all caps be sure to do the same for the other sections. Consistency errors can sink a resume faster than a misspelled word. Why? Errors are distracting, and once one error is found, the reviewer will either compare your resume to others to see how many exist before tossing your resume or will simply discard your resume.

KEY POINTS OF REFERENCE:

The first thing you need to do when storyboarding your resume is to draft your contact information.

After that is complete, focus on the 3 by 3 format starting with the first three items known as the front matter, which appears at the top of the resume after your contact heading:

1. Headline
2. Summary
3. Core Skills

The second three items follow and include:

1. Experience
2. Education
3. Other

Tailor your content based on the job you are applying for, using the job posting as a guide. Be sure to use action verbs in the proper tense. Stay away from outdated phrases and overused words. Use proper grammar and be consistent always.

PLAN OF ACTION:

Start drafting your resume. Remember, there are a couple of example resumes in the back of this book, and templates available by accessing the bonus material. Also, if the illustrations in this chapter were difficult to read, remember a document with larger images is included in your free bonus materials too. Access to bonus materials can be found in the back of this book under the section heading called Thank You – Free Gift (Bonus Materials).

WORDS OF WISDOM:

The only way to begin the process is to start.

9

MOVING FORWARD

As you move forward in your job search, it is essential to remember the real purpose of the resume. The resume is to be used as a tactical marketing document that demonstrates your true value to a potential employer. It is not meant to be a long diatribe of your entire work history. It is not even supposed to be a summary of your whole career.

As a marketing document, your resume must be up-to-date whether or not you are searching for a new job. There are times that you will need to use a resume outside of job searching:

- Networking
- Internal Promotion Opportunities

- Speaking Engagements
- Award Recognition
- Board Positions
- Volunteer Positions

The more senior you are in your career, the more important it is to have a ready-to-go resume.

A good time to consider updating your resume is before your annual assessment/performance review. You are sharing your accomplishments during the review so add them to your resume while they are fresh and top of mind. Updating your resume will allow for some good self-assessment, which can provide valuable insight to discuss during your annual review.

Having an updated resume is also a good way to communicate your value and your brand at a moment's notice. You don't want to be scrambling and feeling overwhelmed, trying to throw something together on short notice.

You will know when the time is right to seek out a new position. There will be telltale signs: high turnover rate, a bad outcome from a merger, or unfavorable changes due to new leadership.

As you review your resume in preparation for future jobs, look at your resume through the proper lens. Consider the following:

- **Is my resume optimized for skimmers?** Remember, reviewers are looking at hundreds of resumes at a time and the higher up in the chain your resume goes, the less time they have to spend on reviewing it. Seriously, if you are at the senior level in your career and you are looking to gain a C-suite position, imagine how much time a C-suite executive has to review your resume. Unfortunately, not much time at all.

The same goes for the new college graduate applying for paid internships or their first career position. How many other graduates do you think are trying for those same jobs? A lot! Truth be told, the numbers are staggering. I remember the first time I realized how many graduates existed when I was working for a law school in Southeast Virginia. I compiled the data and shared the job placement rates for all graduating law students every year. As I was compiling the information, I received an industry report that maintained the numbers for all accredited law schools in the United States, which at the time was 188. The report revealed 42,672 law students graduated in that year alone. If that is just law schools, can you imagine how many individuals are graduating from more than 31,000 accredited post-secondary institutions annually?

What is the point? You need to optimize your resume to help you make it through the noise and stand out against the competition.

- **Did I incorporate enough keywords throughout my resume?** Keywords are those words that are relevant to your target roles. To find the right keywords, go to the job listing. As you review the listing, highlight the words that stand out. Those are the words you place in the core skills area of your resume and incorporate into your bulleted items in the Experience section.

Do not get carried away with keyword stuffing. If you pack your resume with too many keywords, the applicant tracking systems will recognize it, so it is better to add a few to your core skills area and focus on using them in supporting bulleted items with quantifiable results for highlighting evidence of your true experience.

- **Did I format my resume correctly?**
  The format you choose is important
  because you need to tell your complete
  story in a way that will demonstrate
  your value to a prospective employer
  without doing a complete data dump on
  paper. Chronological is the most
  traditional approach but not always the
  best to use, especially if you have a lot
  of gaps in your resume. A combination
  resume is often best if you have more
  senior level experience, while a
  functional version would be better if you
  are a recent graduate. Read through your
  resume—or better yet, have someone
  else read through your resume and ask
  them what they got out of it. See if what
  they tell you aligns with your intent.

- **Did I target my resume for the role I
  am applying to?** Just because you have
  a solid resume that is branded correctly
  doesn't mean you stop adjusting for
  each role you apply to. You should view
  that resume as a prototype, your
  template for building out for each
  position. You should change up things

slightly to always paint the picture that you are the perfect person for the job.

If you remember the points I have shared, you will be ready when an opportunity presents itself and will not become overwhelmed when someone requests your resume on a moment's notice.

KEY POINTS OF REFERENCE:

Have a ready-to-go-resume at all times for opportunities outside of job searching. There are plenty of times when a resume is needed. Resumes are often asked for after networking events, for speaking engagements, recognizing individuals for awards, and even for serving on boards.

Prepare your resume by confirming it is optimized for skimmers by reinforcing appropriate keywords, proper formatting, and necessary targeting.

PLAN OF ACTION:

Review your resume and ask yourself the following questions.

- Is my resume optimized for skimming?
- Does my resume contain enough keywords?
- Is my resume in the best format to highlight my value?
- Is my resume targeted to the role for which I am applying?

WORDS OF WISDOM:

For this chapter, a military statement comes to mind: "Proper planning prevents poor performance." If you take the necessary time to prepare your resume as outlined, you will find that the job search process is not that overwhelming. You will be ready and your resume will stand out in the mind of the reviewer.

III

YOUR MINDSET

GET YOUR MIND RIGHT

A frequent issue people deal with when forced to write a resume is not what you would think. It is not spelling errors, conveying misinformation, or having poor design quality. Those don't arise as much as having the right mindset. As discussed in Part II of this book, grammar, content, and design are essential, but the focus of this chapter is a bit different.

The most common issue has more to do with your mindset to maintain a positive attitude than anything else. If you do not have the right mindset when starting the job hunt, you will find the entire process to be an uphill battle. It will not only be hard to move forward but even harder to stay motivated and keep your thoughts in check. Often the reason a person is seeking a new job dictates their mindset.

There are many reasons people look for a new job:

- Career growth
- Downsizing
- Mergers
- Layoffs
- Toxic environments
- Boredom
- Military transition

The list is not all-inclusive, but you get the point. People start the job quest for many reasons. Individuals who need to find a new job as a result of circumstances outside of their control often feel rejected. This can cause them to have a bad attitude, which will arise when discussing the situation for their departure. Sometimes a bad attitude arises even when the person is in control of the entire job search process. The point of this chapter is simply to ensure you have the right mindset so that you can experience the best outcome, which is a job that you are thrilled to go to every day, making the money you deserve.

How do you get your mindset right? To have a

good attitude, you must focus not on your circumstances, but rather on the new opportunities that will be open to you. Look at everything you have to offer. You are a talented individual with great skills, and those skills are transferable. It doesn't matter what happened at the previous company because they do not determine your worth, you do. You are in complete control of what happens going forward, which brings me to the issue of negativity.

Negativity feeds a bad attitude. Perhaps you are feeling negative because of the reason you were let go or left your job, even if it was on your terms. It could be that you were passed up for a promotion and decided to leave to move forward elsewhere, or maybe it was related to a toxic situation. No matter the reason, negativity hurts you.

How does it hurt you? When you possess a negative/pessimistic outlook, your resume tone will carry it too. If you make it to an interview, you may not put your best foot forward either. For instance, you could be distracted and miss important body language cues, answer questions wrong, become defensive, or even bad talk your former employer. Worse, you could come across as a victim.

Pages 102 - 104 provides and example of a true scenario I encountered recently.

A client contacted me in desperation. She was stuck in a toxic environment, which was causing her to respond negatively to everything I said. After several minutes she broke down crying. She apologized for being so pessimistic and explained that she felt as though she was at the triage phase of her situation. In her mind, the situation she was dealing with equated to a serious crisis. She was retiring from the Navy Reserve in less than six months and she could no longer tolerate her civilian job. The tough part was that she felt alone. She was single and responsible for her financial well-being. She had no savings and, to make matters worse, she had hired a resume writer who kept trying to sell her on the idea of a five-page resume. She was confused and desperate, which caused her to feel hopeless.

Have you ever found yourself in a situation where you felt hopeless? I know I have, and it was not a fun place to be. It is overwhelming and drains the life out of you.

To help her breathe easy, I reminded her that she was in control of her situation.

To help her take control back, she needed to do a couple of things. First, her resume needed a formal review. Second, she needed to work on changing her mindset. Easy to say, I know, but it can be done. To change her mindset, she needed to change how she envisioned things. For example, as a kid, I played softball. I was too old to play tee-ball or coach pitch, so I was forced to learn how to hit. My dad always told me to envision the bat hitting the ball. It sounds simplistic, but it also works. I followed his guidance, and by the time the teenage years rolled around, I was known as a clean-up hitter. Envisioning a particular outcome can be similar when it comes to searching for a new job. Seeing yourself getting that new job can change your mindset. Solomon talks about this mindset in Proverbs 17:22 (NIV) when he writes, "A joyful heart is good medicine, but a crushed spirit dries up the bones."

For my client, she had to envision a new outcome for herself. Instead of letting the issue at work crush her spirit, I had her write down all of the things that would bring her joy in her next job. Where would the job be located, what would she do, how much would she make. Little by little the co-workers who were difficult and the supervisor who was a bully didn't matter as much. This bought her a bit more time to plan her escape because she no longer felt desperate. She changed her mindset and focused her energy on changing her outcome.

As for the resume, she used my feedback to

craft a resume that helped her move on to a position better suited for her.

Please do not misunderstand me, I am not suggesting anyone stay in a toxic environment where they are mistreated. If you have the means to leave, I highly recommend for your sanity and safety, you leave. However, if that option is not available, you do not have to give up control. You can control the way you think so that you focus on a better outcome. In doing so, the positive goals you set as you look ahead to a better future will drive you to want to do more to expedite the process.

KEY POINTS OF REFERENCE:

- Make sure you have the right attitude when seeking a new job as this will make the process of finding that job much easier
- Focus on positivity, not negativity as you move forward in the job search process. When you are positive, you find opportunities but when you are negative everything feels like a challenge
- Being negative while working on your

resume could result in a resume with a negative tone
- Bad attitudes and negativity will be felt in an interview

PLAN OF ACTION:

- Do some self-reflection. Are you in the right frame of mind to start the job hunt?
- If you are not in the right frame of mind, determine the reason. If the reason is due to a situation outside of your control, work on things that will give you control back. A good way to start is by giving yourself small goals to accomplish to help you feel like you are moving forward. The goals can be as simple as making a list of your skills and then reading them out loud to remind yourself of your talent and worth.

WORDS OF WISDOM:

The job search process is hard, so it is critical to get your mind right. As Winston Churchill said, "The pessimist sees the difficulty in every opportunity; the optimist sees the opportunity in every difficulty." It is hard to see the opportunities when you have your head down. Get your mind right and stay focused so you don't miss anything!

11

ANXIETY UNWARRANTED

There are so many things that cause anxiety and for many individuals, having to write a resume is one of them. Your resume is not the only thing that will get you the job. Yes, it is important for getting your foot in the door—in fact, you need a resume to land the interview, but that's it. Once you have gotten the interview, you will need your resume only if you apply for another job or apply to serve on a board, volunteer for an organization, or receive an award. Therefore, the anxiety you may have is not warranted. Why? You now have a guide to show you how to do it right. Just as you plan any other task, you have learned how to plan for your resume too.

In this book, you learned exactly what I did to help others create resumes that landed them not one interview but several. Those interviews led to some pretty great six-figure salaries. The even better part is that my clients were always in control. They determined which job they ultimately took, and you will be able to do the same.

As I mentioned in the previous chapter, having the right mindset is critical. If you are anxious, you will also experience negative outcomes. Philippians 4:6 tells us, "Do not be anxious about anything." Instead, focus on the plan and know that the right doors will open because you are doing the right things.

You learned how to design your resume to highlight the skills sought after in the job for which you are applying. You are interviewing the companies as much as they are interviewing you. You do not need to feel desperate as if that is the only job you must take.

Think about the times you have felt anxious. Usually, the reason we feel anxious is that there is uncertainty; we fear the unknown or we don't like change. In this situation, you are in control of the job quest. You are in control of how your resume looks, and you are in control of the companies and jobs you choose to explore.

You may say, "I have applied to many jobs through online job sites, but nothing has popped so when do I worry?" I don't doubt that you have applied to many online jobs. There could be several reasons why you didn't receive a call. Many job sites proudly promote they receive several resumes a minute. A prominent one touts that they receive 29 resumes a minute, or about 15 million a year. Wow, that is a lot of competition! Granted, you are not applying to every single job on their site, but it still demonstrates the large number of people you have to compete with when applying online. Don't let this make you anxious, instead change the way you look for jobs.

Did you know that networking is the best way to get jobs and that 85% of the jobs are never advertised? They are shared through connections. The possibility of getting a job would be much greater going the networking route than the online job site route.

Friends, I will end this chapter and this section of the book with a note on mindset. Although some may wonder why I chose to talk about mindset it is important to recognize that if your mind is distracted for any reason it will roll over into other areas. It is important to remind you that God is in control of your life. Like others, you may have to deal with work-life realities that may not be fun, but God is still in control. Once you get your mind right, the job quest goes so much easier. "Trust in the Lord with all your heart and lean not on your own understanding." (Proverbs 3:5 NIV). You will not be anxious and you may even find the job hunt enjoyable like doing a puzzle where you make all the pieces fit. The pieces will fit.

KEY POINTS OF REFERENCE:

- Anxiety is unwarranted when you have a plan in place for a successful outcome
- You are in control of how you choose to move forward in the job quest

PLAN OF ACTION:

- If there is anything you are anxious about, write it down. Look at the reasons you have written down and determine which ones you have control over and which ones must be turned over to God.

WORDS OF WISDOM:

You do not need to feel anxious about your resume. According to Pat Riley, "Great effort springs naturally from a great attitude." Having a great attitude is half the battle.

12

WRAP UP: GET SEEN, GET HIRED, GET PAID

This book was broken down into three parts —your message, your story, and your mindset—for a very important reason. To get seen, get hired, and get paid, you have to prepare. As you learned, preparing requires the right mindset. I have helped hundreds of people at all levels find jobs. I can tell you with certainty that individuals with a positive mindset get jobs a lot faster than those who have a pessimistic attitude. I understand what it feels like to send out resume after resume with no response or to receive a rejection letter for a job you were perfectly qualified for. The job search can be tough and it doesn't get any easier if you have tons of experience; however, it gets a lot easier when you stay positive and learn how to communicate your worth effectively.

Translating your experience in a way that conveys your message appropriately is key. It is no different than a company trying to sell a new product. Companies use specific words to convince consumers that they can't live without that product. It is the same process you need to go through to get a reviewer to choose you over hundreds of other applicants.

Have a resume on hand when an opportunity comes knocking. If you prepare your resume before you need it, you have time to work on your core message, which comes alive through story-telling. The story unfolds as you share details about your experiences and connect them to the role for which you are applying. The story is not made up of fiction but contributions you made to your current and former employers and the accomplishments that went along with those efforts. As you plot your story for each position, you can start to brand yourself as an expert in a particular area. This is a key tactic to separate yourself from the competition. You are unique and although others may do the same job, they will never have the same story of how they did it. People applying for the same position will most likely list bullet points that provide task information, which won't set them apart.

You can further develop your story by learning more about your audience so that you know who you are targeting. It is also important to know the audience so that you know what professional language they speak. As a management consultant, my first big client was NASA. After four years on the job providing advice to NASA, I was sent to the Navy. Initially, it was a bit of a culture shock. Both organizations were acronym heavy, but the acronyms did not mean the same thing. The language used in general was very different. As a strategic communicator, I needed to learn to speak the language of the Navy if I were to excel. You will need to speak the language of your prospective employer, and the only way to do that on your resume is to know who your audience is so that you can do some research on them.

Mindset and message are how you get seen, but presentation is how you get hired and paid. This is where the second section on resume development is critical. You need to breathe new life into your old resume, and that starts with understanding what you are expected to know when it comes to the modern format. A perfect example is noting on your resume you are tech-savvy but neglecting to create a tailored LinkedIn profile URL in your contact heading.

Another dead giveaway that you are not keeping up with technology is if you include an objective on your resume. Everyone knows the objective is to get a job, so you waste valuable resume real estate and look like a resume rookie when you use it. You want to include a value statement in a summary on your modern resume to help you stand out. Finally, the fonts you use are tell-tale signs to a reviewer if you are Microsoft Word smart. Use anything but a universal font and the reviewer might toss your resume without reading it.

Designing your resume in a way that meets the new rules while also being visually appealing is how you get paid because you are demonstrating your worth of the salary you seek.

Below are some quick reminders to keep you on the right track.

Don't be a needle in a haystack. Most resumes are read by an audience short on time. Stress your points upfront; do not make your resume reader hunt for skills. Also, do not highlight upfront your accomplishments without connecting them to specific jobs. This is where the 3 by 3 format helps.

Headlines aid reviewers in sizing up the candidate in seconds. Keep it tight, lean, and clean with content only, not unwarranted personal details, career objectives, etc.

A blurb, not a Bible. I am a Christian and love to read the Bible, but not when I am trying to decipher a resume. The point of the resume is to tell me a little bit about you so that I am motivated to call you in for an interview. The resume is not meant to contain your life history. Share only items relevant to the role to which you are applying.

No exaggerations. Being less than forthcoming, hiding gaps between roles, listing a degree you worked towards but did not complete, or fudging job titles are all ways to get yourself in trouble. I have heard and echo the sentiments of employers who have said, "if the initial conversation is not based on trust, there's no question of its conversion into an offer!" Don't risk losing out on a great opportunity by conveniently leaving out something important, especially since most employers want to hire talented people despite gaps or in progress degrees. It is easy to include additional information in the cover letter and to explain a situation further in the interview.

KEY POINTS OF REFERENCE:

Getting seen, getting hired, and getting paid requires effort. It starts with your message, your story, and your mindset. You need to prepare in advance to ensure the resume you create is tailored for the right audience and you need to follow the rules so that you don't look like a resume rookie.

PLAN OF ACTION:

- Review the chapters in this book to ensure you have not missed anything
- Review the sample resumes and other free resources by going to http:// bit.ly/breatheresume

WORDS OF WISDOM:

I agree with Abraham Lincoln's quote, "Always bear in mind that your own resolution to succeed is more important than any other." You have been equipped with the information to produce an effective resume; however, it will ultimately come down to your motivation for moving forward to make things happen.

I will be cheering for you as you move forward on your journey to finding the perfect position!

Sincerely,
Jeannine

ACKNOWLEDGMENTS

Thank you to my husband, Hayden for always encouraging me to write and work with others sometimes at the cost of spending time with him. He is my best friend and my constant support.

To Jim Murphy and Rebekah Woods who hired me all those years ago to serve in the Career and Alumni Services Department at Regent University. Although it has been years since we all worked together, I am grateful for the opportunity that ultimately led to my calling.

To my wonderful co-workers, while at Regent, who were always such a source of encouragement: Lisa Marie Otto, Lisa Rothwell, Mary Bunch, Susan

Stewart, Holly Miller, Marie Markham, Laura Hanson, Carol Ann Dick, Kathy Stull, Donna Cunningham, and many others.

Most of all thank you to my God who gave me life and a purpose!

ABOUT THE AUTHOR

Dr. Jeannine Bennett is an author, and the Founder and CEO of Vision to Purpose, located in Virginia Beach, Virginia. She is also an adjunct faculty member in the School of Business at Liberty University, and an executive coach for the Honor Foundation, an organization dedicated to helping special operators find positions after service. She has more than 30 years of experience working in different roles in various industries to include: academia, business, government, law, media, and tech.

Jeannine's love for all things career-related began in 1998 when she worked in the Career and Alumni Services Department at Regent University's School of Law. Helping law students and alumni find positions fueled a passion that later could not be quenched in any other role she held. No matter where she worked or what she was doing she kept up with career trends and continued to help individuals reach their career goals. The desire to help individuals move forward in their career endeavors is what ultimately led Jeannine to make the hard decision to leave federal government service to focus full-time on her calling. Her "why" as they say is "To be a light for others so they can find their way." Her why drives everything she does no matter the role: entrepreneur, coach, educator, wife, mother or grandmother.

She has been blessed with the opportunity to live out her passion by helping thousands of people through her contributions as an educator for degree-seeking students and as an entrepreneur offering direct support to clients seeking her assistance. To date, she has helped individuals at all levels in their career journey from entry-level high school and college graduates to middle career and executive-level seasoned professionals. Her clients have been as diverse as the positions they seek. They are students, educators, stellar athletes (Olympians, Ironmen, World Champions), military members and veterans from all service branches with varied backgrounds (aviators, special operators, etc.), educators, lawyers, IT and cyber experts, doctors, nurses, sales professionals, the list goes on.

Jeannine is what you would call a scholar-practitioner possessing both an M.B.A. and a Ph.D. and certifications as well as experience in different fields. She values family and her most important roles include being a wife to Hayden, and a mom to three children and grandmother to six grandchildren.

You can follow Jeannine on LinkedIn at www.linkedin.com/in/jbennettphd/ and by signing up for the Vision to Purpose newsletter at https://visiontopurpose.com/newsletter/.

ABOUT VISION TO PURPOSE

Vision to Purpose is a Christian organization dedicated to helping individuals, and organizations succeed through the offering of tailored career, life and business solutions. Some of the services offered by Vision to Purpose include:

- Career Assessment
- Career and Life Coaching
- Resume and Cover Letter Writing
- Job Search Strategies and Interview Prep
- Leadership Development
- Professional Development
- Copy Writing
- Strategic Communications

- Speech Writing
- Public Speaking
- Project Management, and more…

To learn more about Vision to Purpose, visit www.visiontopurpose.com.

If you want to receive messages daily, please connect with us on Facebook at www.facebook.com/VisiontoPurpose/ or follow us on LinkedIn www. linkedin.com/company/vision-to-purpose/

SIGN UP FOR THE
NEWSLETTER

At Vision to Purpose we have helped hundreds of professionals gain employment, make career changes and progress in their careers. Through the offering of coaching, resume writing, career-focused courses and shared community we equip individuals with the tools they need to be successful in their careers. We would like to do the same for you. Please sign up for the Vision to Purpose newsletter to stay connected and to keep receiving information to assist you in growing your career to the level you desire.

In the newsletter you will receive:

- Latest Insights
- Career Tips & Strategies
- Best Practices
- Expert Advice Resources
- Discounts on Services
- Job Leads and much more!

Go to https://visiontopurpose.com/newsletter/ to start receiving the monthly Vision to Purpose newsletter today.

THANK YOU - FREE GIFT -
BONUS MATERIALS

As my way of saying thank you for your purchase, I would like to offer you some free bonus materials.

This bonus package contains sample resumes to review, resume templates to use, discounted resume e-course access, a resume checklist and a list of action verbs. You can access your free bonus materials here: http://bit.ly/breatheresume

SAMPLE RESUME 1 - ENTRY LEVEL

SALLY SAMPLE

123 Anywhere Court, Any Town, IL 12345 • Phone: (123) 456-7891 • Email: sallysample@aol.com

OFFICE OPERATIONS & MANAGEMENT PROFESSIONAL

10 years of business experience specializing in bookkeeping and property management. Relate warmly to diverse individuals at all levels by using a friendly yet confident communication style. Possess excellent time and resource management skills.

Bookkeeping Expertise:
- Office Operations
- Accounts Payables/Receivables
- Payroll
- Tax and Insurance Management
- Document Preparation
- Customer Calls

Property Management Experience:
- Tenant Relations & Retention
- Collections
- Negotiation
- Conflict Resolution
- Maintenance and Renovation
- Contractor Management

RELEVANT WORK EXPERIENCE

123 Trucking Bookkeeping, Any Town, VA   07/2013 - Present
Bookkeeper for Trucking Company

- Utilize Peachtree (Sage50) Accounting Software
- Manage cash flow, customer payments, and collections
- Perform essential accounting: accounts receivable, accounts payable, payroll

Best Trucking Bookkeeping, Any Town, VA   09/2005 - 03/2012
Bookkeeper for Trucking Company

- Made specialized purchases, drafted receipts and ensured payments
- Organized and established office operations and procedures
- Reviewed time sheets, maintained logbooks and prepared payroll
- Maintained all records and logbooks for tax purposes; made monthly and quarterly tax payments

Awesome Property Management, Any Town, VA   04/2001 - 06/2005
Assistant Property Manager

- Showed properties to prospective tenants, negotiating rental agreements
- Evaluated credit reports of clients and conducted background checks
- Scheduled maintenance and renovations with responsibility to oversee contractors
- Resolved disputes including evictions, payment demands, deposit demands, etc.
- Maintained client and property database
- Promoted from a Leasing Agent to Assistant Manager

ENTREPRENEURIAL EXPERIENCE

A Cleaning Service, Anytown, VA   09/2002 - 09/2004
Owner

- Established business and increased clientele to 12 residential and commercial accounts
- Provided thorough cleaning for offices and homes
- Maintained business accounting and tax preparations

SPECIALIZED SKILLS

- Microsoft Office Suite: Word, PowerPoint, Excel

Figure 22. Entry Level Sample Resume

Note: For a larger, more detailed view of this resume please see the free bonus materials. Both sample resumes are included in that package.

SAMPLE RESUME 2 - PROFESSIONAL LEVEL

SALLY SAMPLE   123.456.7890 – SSAMPLE@GMAIL.COM – CITY, STATE

**PROGRAM
MANAGEMENT /
COMMUNICATION
SPECIALIST**

- Seasoned professional adept at strategic communications planning and implementation
- Charismatic and creative communication expert with a track record of delivering tailored messages to the right audience at the right time using the right channel
- Forward-thinking program manager skilled at overseeing and guiding large programs dedicated to providing support to the public

SPOTLIGHTED SUCCESS

Program / PR /Communication Accomplishments
- Directed the planning and implementation of statewide advocacy programs typically reaching 350+ Directed the planning and implementation of statewide advocacy programs reaching 350+ attendees
- Recruited, trained and mobilized 600 community activists via legislative advocacy and campus organizing to carry out communications strategies designed to address public policy goals
- Garnered over 75 earned media hits in print, television and via radio
- Designed and executed 25 volunteer training sessions on topics pertaining to message development, media engagement, lobbying, and community outreach

PROFESSIONAL EXPERIENCE

State Department of Education, City, State   2017 - Present
School Nutrition Programs Coordinator
Serves as the program manager for two highly visible, complex Federal child nutrition programs and the project coordinator for the planning and implementation of the new management information system. Develops policies and procedures for administration of the Summer Food Service Program and At-Risk Afterschool Meals Program. Liaises with Office of the First Lady of Virginia and Virginia No Kid Hungry initiative. Supervises a small staff, talented staff of four individuals.

Key Accomplishments:
- Hand selected by the Governor of Virginia to transition from the State Department of Health to the State Department of Education

State Department of Health, City, State   2012 - 2014; 2015 - 2017
Special Nutrition Programs Certification and Training Supervisor
Special Nutrition Programs Liaison (03/2012 - 05/2014)
Oversaw application process for Child and Adult Care Food Program (CACFP) and Summer Food Service Program (SFSP), including screening, training, and approval processes. Developed and executed programmatic training sessions and webinars for program participants. Analyzed and interpreted federal regulations and policy memos for both programs. Supervised a staff of four (4) program specialists. Managed relationships with diverse groups of stakeholders to ensure food insecure populations receive quality, nutritious meals.

Key Accomplishments:
- Provided customer service and technical assistance to 400 sponsoring organizations: nonprofits, school systems, governmental entities, and military installations
- Directed State Department of Health's portion of the State 365 Project, an $8.8 million USDA demonstration grant to end childhood hunger
- Managed rollout and training of management information system statewide
- Conducted compliance reviews of entities receiving CACFP and SFSP funding; synthesized review findings and communicated with program participants to ensure compliance with federal regulations

Figure 23. Professional Level Sample Resume Front Page

Advocacy Center, City, State   2014 - 2015
Director of Media Relations
Served as the spokesperson for the Advocacy Center. Oversaw the development of marketing initiatives and defined, tracked, measured and reported on the progress of those initiatives against organizational goals.

Key Accomplishments:
- Cultivated relationships with members of the media in collaboration with coalition partners
- Coordinated and executed comprehensive media relations strategies to advance the organization's brand and health care services
- Developed messaging and media materials: press releases, opinion editorials, letters to the editor, fact sheets, web site and social media content. Implemented crisis communications plans when needed
- Created targeted advertisements for various communication channels and audiences: direct mail pieces, brochures, t-shirts, yard signs and banners
- Established systems and work plans for orderly workflow process and to ensure a high level of customer service satisfaction among colleagues seeking collaboration on communications projects
- Trained organizational spokespersons: patients, medical professionals, and community leaders

League for the Advocacy Center, City, State   2005 - 2012
Public Affairs Manager
Served as spokesperson for the League for the Advocacy Center, chair of Lobby Day planning committee and active member of statewide coalitions.

Key Accomplishments:
- Directed crisis communications response in consultation with the Advocacy Center of America
- Generated content and user guidelines for organizational website and social media platforms
- Managed email communication system to send action alerts to over 20,000 members
- Developed annual grant proposals and compiled quarterly reports for grant-funded work using qualitative and quantitative measures for efficacy of program
- Directed the planning and implementation of statewide advocacy programs, i.e. Lobby Day at Virginia General Assembly (350+ attendees), and student leadership conferences
- Recruited, trained, and mobilized 600 community activists to carry out public policy goals
- Designed and executed 25 training sessions on: messaging, media, lobbying, and community outreach

EDUCATION

Commonwealth University, City, State   2014
Master of Public Administration, Concentration in Nonprofit Management

Prominent University, City, State   2003
Bachelor of Arts in English

CORE SKILLS

- Program Oversight
- Media & Public Relations
- Communication Management
- Writing & Editing
- Presentation Development
- Research & Data Analysis
- Multimedia Communication
- Brand Communication
- Relationship Building
- Microsoft Office Programs
- Social Media Platforms

PROFESSIONAL DEVELOPMENT

State Department of Health, City, State   2016 - 2017
Emerging Leaders Program

Nonprofit Learning Point, City, State   2011
Marketing 101 for Nonprofits

Nonprofit Learning Point, City, State   2010 - 2011
Emerging Nonprofit Leaders Program

Figure 24. Professional Level Sample Resume Back Page

ADDITIONAL
RECOMMENDATIONS

"Jeannine is absolutely amazing! Her knowledge of military and ability to translate our terminology into civilian culture has been absolutely crucial in my transition. At this high-stress pivot point in my life, Jeannine has been a shining star of inspiration and mentorship guiding me through the process, I can honestly never thank her enough!" *Brandon, transitioning Navy SEAL, Military*

"I was searching for someone to help me update my resume and I found Jeannine through LinkedIn ProFinder. I clicked with Jeannine right away and felt as if I had known her forever. Jeannine helped me figure out how to translate my skills into a career path through her coaching. She also enhanced my

LinkedIn page and offered expert advice along the way. Jeannine was professional and did exactly what she said she would do. I highly recommend her if you need a resume writer, a career coach or a LinkedIn specialist. My experience with Jeannine was both professional and pleasant."
Ruth, Facebook Business Operations Coordinator, Technology Industry

"Jeannine reviewed my resume and gave me solid recommendations and concrete examples. She showed me what a successful skills resume looks like and I used her analysis to revamp my resume. When I posted my new version, I got two inquiries in 24 hours, one leading to an interview."
Mike, Public Affairs Officer, Government Sector

"I wanted to let you know that the resume you did for me and some networking landed me a phone interview, then a google hangout interview and today I had my face to face. I got the job!" *Arinn, Career Services Instructor, Higher Education Industry*

"I simply cannot say enough good things about Jeannine Bennett with Vision to Purpose! She was exceptionally thorough, surprising me with her independent research; this was easily the best investment I have ever made in myself! When I read the initial draft, I honestly couldn't believe it was ME described on paper, but yet there it was - my accomplishments and talents presented in impressive fashion. I can't recommend Jeannine highly enough, and definitely, plan on keeping her contact information at arm's reach." *Gina, Account Cultivation Management, Oil & Gas Industry*

"From start to finish everything was done professionally and with perfection. If you need a resume written I would highly recommend Vision to Purpose! They will make you shine! Job well done!" *Eugenia, Nonprofit Executive Director, Social Service Industry*

"I was looking for an expert to help create a compelling resume and equivalent LinkedIn profile that properly reflected my passion and interests in cloud technology. I received several offers on LinkedIn but decided to go with Jeannine because of her thoughtful questions and helpful suggestions ... indeed, her professionalism struck me from day one! And in less than two weeks, Jeannine created a very appealing LinkedIn page and top notch resume. The thing I really appreciated about Jeannine, in addition to her superb creativity and skills, was her ability to truly "listen" to my needs, interpret them, use her resourcefulness in creating multiple options (mockups) to choose from, and finish it up with excellent results! It was very evident that Jeannine truly cares for each client individually and loves her tradecraft. I feel very blessed to have found and worked with Jeannine. You'll be happy you did too! I wholeheartedly recommend Jeannine for your career branding and coaching needs."

Conrad, Cloud Development and Security Leader, Not-for-Profit Research Sector

ONLINE RESUME COURSE

Coming Soon

The **Breathe Life into Your Resume Online Course** is in progress and will be available on January 1, 2020. The course not only covers topics discussed in the book but includes exercises and videos to guide you through your resume development.

You will be able to access the course here:

http://bit.ly/Breatheresumecourse

The course will cost $99; however, as readers of the book, you get a huge discount. Below is the code to use to get the course for $29.

Code: BREATHE